Transfer and Stitch

Butterflies, Bees and Bugs

OVER 50 REUSABLE MOTIFS TO IRON ON AND EMBROIDER

Sally McCollin

SEARCH PRESS

First published in 2018

Search Press Limited
Wellwood, North Farm Road,
Tunbridge Wells, Kent TN2 3DR

Stitch illustrations by Bess Harding: pages 9–13; with the
exception of 'whipped backstitch', supplied by Sally McCollin

Photographs by Paul Bricknell at Search Press Studios

ISBN: 978-1-78221-323-9

Suppliers

All of the wonderful embroidery threads and Desire Memory
Wires were kindly supplied by DMC Creative World. To find
your local stockist, visit: www.dmccreative.co.uk

If you have any difficulty obtaining any of the materials
and equipment mentioned in this book, please visit the
Search Press website: www.searchpress.com

Publisher's note

The designs within this book were created by the author,
Sally McCollin. One of the designs featured in this book has
been adapted from the following title, previously published by
Search Press:

Design Source Book: Classic Border Designs by Judy Balchin.

**Please note: to remove the transfers you want to use from
the book, cut round them carefully. They can be stored in
the pocket at the back of the book and used several times.**

Dedication

I would like to dedicate this book to anyone
who is supporting a family member suffering
from dementia. It can be heartbreaking
and frustrating at times to see a once-
independent, intelligent person forever
changed by this disease. It is teaching me to
slow down and be more patient.

Acknowledgements

I would like to thank Cara Ackerman of
DMC Creative World for supplying such a
wonderful array of threads. I think I should
also thank my husband, Martin, for his
patience and understanding when regularly
faced with the biggest mess that I could
possibly make.

The designs in this book were inspired by
visits to butterfly farms based at Dalkeith
and at Preston Park.

Printed in China through Asia Pacific Offset

Satin stitch

Satin stitch is good for filling small areas quickly. The stitches look best worked closely together and the effect can be particularly pleasing if a variegated thread is used. By adjusting the length of the stitches it can be worked to fit most shapes. Take care when placing your needle so that you get an even edge.

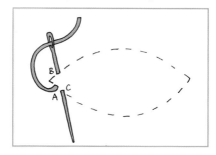 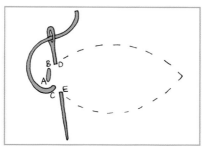 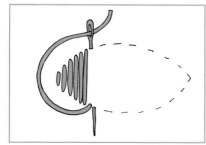

1 Bring your thread up at A, on the edge of the shape, and insert the needle at B. Pull the thread through gently. Pulling the thread too tightly will cause the fabric to pucker. Bring the needle up at C, working as close to A as possible.

2 Take the needle down at D, as close as possible to B, and bring it back through at E, next to C. Pull the thread through gently to make a stitch that lies next to the first stitch, without overlapping it.

3 Continue as above until the shape is filled. Pass the needle through to the back of the work to fasten off. You may find it easier to work one half of the shape at a time, working from the centre out to each side.

Stem stitch

Stem stitch makes a lovely smooth, unbroken line. It can be worked as an outline stitch or as a filling stitch, when rows are laid down close together.

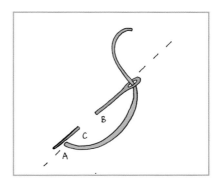 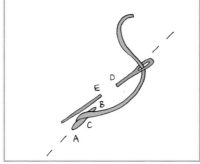 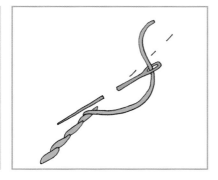

1 Bring the thread through at A and hold it down with your thumb to form a loop. Insert the needle at B and bring it out at C, between A and B.

2 Pull the thread through to make the first stitch. Hold the working thread down with your thumb as before. Insert the needle at D and bring it out at E, slightly to the side of B.

3 Continue until the line of stitching is complete. If using as a filling stitch, simply work another row next to the first and repeat until the area is filled.

Transferring the designs

The transfer sheets for all the designs are at the back of the book. You can cut around the parts you want to use individually, but make sure you leave as much paper as possible around the edge. When you have used the transfer, store it in the pocket on the back cover to keep it safe until you wish to use it again. Transfer the designs using an ordinary iron (without steam) set on 'cotton'. Make sure you use a fabric that won't be damaged by this heat. If possible, use a spare piece of your fabric to check before you start.

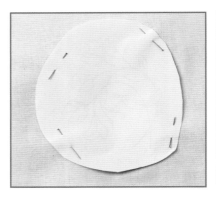

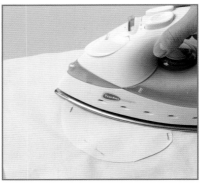

1 Pin the transfer ink-side down on the right side of the fabric where you want the design to be.

2 Place the iron over the transfer area and leave for about ten seconds. Do not move the iron, as this may blur the image. Carefully lift a corner of the transfer to make sure it has printed on to the fabric. If not, leave the iron for a little longer or increase the temperature and try again.

3 When you are happy that the design has transferred successfully, remove the transfer. Your design is now ready to be placed in the embroidery hoop for stitching.

Using dark and heavily patterned fabrics

If your fabric is dark or has a heavy all-over pattern, it may be hard to see the transferred outline. To overcome this problem, embroider the design on to a piece of plain or lighter-coloured fabric and then sew it on to the darker fabric. Alternatively, the transfer can be ironed on to a water-soluble fabric. This can then be tacked (basted) on to the item to be stitched and washed away when the stitching has been completed.

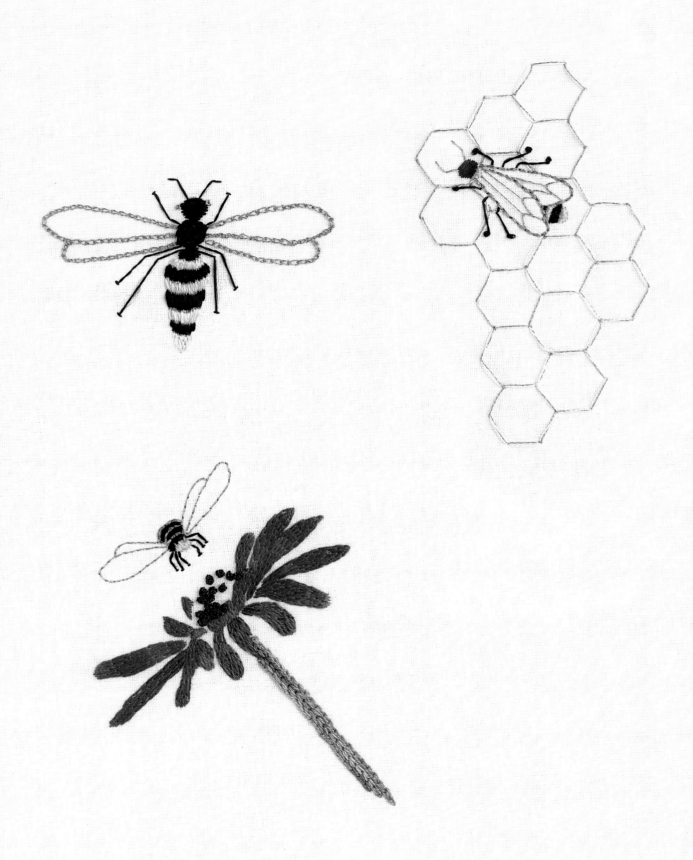

5 Thread key

DMC colours used:

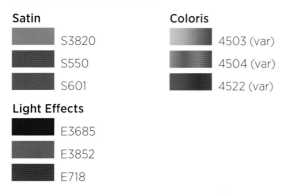

Satin

S3820

S550

S601

Light Effects

E3685

E3852

E718

Coloris

4503 (var)

4504 (var)

4522 (var)

Stitches and threads used for the single bee:

Yellow stripes worked in chain stitch using one strand of S3820. Eye worked in French knots using one strand of S3820.

Dark stripes worked in French knots using one strand of 4504 (var).

Face worked in chain stitch using one strand of 4504 (var).

Legs worked in backstitch using one strand of 4504 (var).

Wings outlined with couching using three strands of E718 couched with one strand of S550.

Flight trail and tips of feelers worked in French knots using one strand of E718.

Stitches and threads used for the bee and flower:

Bee

Gold stripes worked in long and short stitch using two strands of E3852. Wings outlined in backstitch using one strand of E3852.

Dark stripes worked in long and short stitch using two strands of E3685. Body worked in satin stitch using two strands of E3685.

Head worked in satin stitch using one strand of 4522 (var).

Feelers and legs worked in backstitch using one strand of 4504 (var).

Flower

Seed head outlined in backstitch using one strand of 4504 (var) with one strand of S601.

Tendrils worked in backstitch using one strand of 4522 (var).

Tips of tendrils worked in French knots using two strands of E718.

Stem worked in stem stitch using two strands of 4503 (var).

Top of flowerhead worked in French knots using one strand of 4504 (var) mixed with E718.

11 Thread key

DMC colours used:

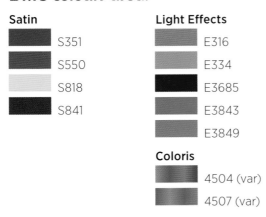

Satin
- S351
- S550
- S818
- S841

Light Effects
- E316
- E334
- E3685
- E3843
- E3849

Coloris
- 4504 (var)
- 4507 (var)

Stitches and threads used on top design:

Upper edges of wings worked in chain stitch using two strands of S351 with one strand of E316.

Tail and lower edges of wings worked in chain stitch using two strands of 4507 (var) with one strand of E3843.

Loop markings on wings worked in backstitch using two strands of E3685.

Line patterns on wings worked in backstitch using two strands of E3849.

Feelers worked in backstitch using two strands of E334.

Purple teardrops worked in satin stitch using two strands of S550 and outlined in lazy daisy stitch using two strands of E316.

Feather markings worked in fly stitch using two strands of E316 with one strand of S818.

Rings at tip of wings worked in blanket stitch using two strands of 4504 (var).

Stitches and threads used on bottom design:

Head and body

Feelers worked in stem stitch using two strands of S550.

Body outlined in backstitch using two strands of S818. Head worked in French knots using two strands of S818.

Marking worked in straight stitch using two strands of E316. Start from the top centre, working stitches alternately from side to side diagonally, keeping them parallel to previous stitches to form a lattice effect.

Upper wings

Wings outlined with couching using three strands of E3685 couched with one strand of S818.

Working from inner edge, where the wings join the body, to the wing tips:

Inner markings worked in satin stitch using two strands of 4504 (var) with one strand of S841.

Lower wings

Wings outlined with couching using three strands of E316 couched with one strand of S841.

Working from inner edge, where the wings join the body, to the wing tips:

Inner markings worked in long and short stitch using two strands of 4504 (var) with one strand of S841.

Wavy patterns worked in satin stitch using two strands of E316.

Dots worked in satin stitch using two strands of S550.

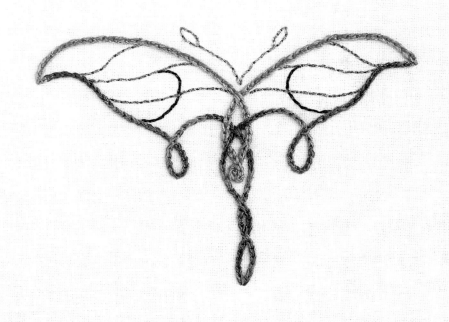

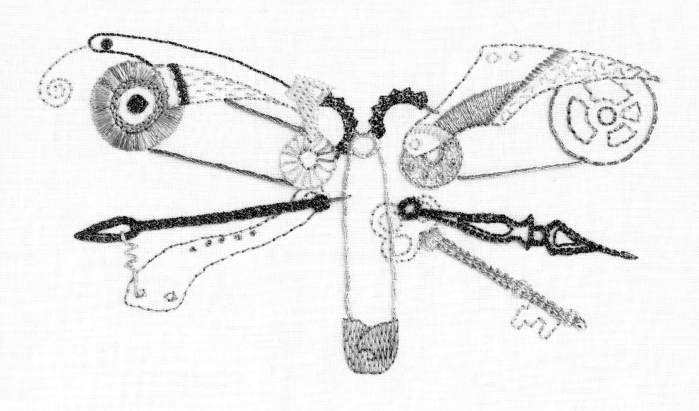

16 Thread key

DMC colours used:

Satin

S321

S367

S472

S606

Light Effects

E130

E321

E825

Coloris

4512 (var)

4517 (var)

Stitches and threads used:

Flowers and stems

 Dark green stems, leaves and bases of flowers outlined in chain stitch using two strands of S367.

Light green stems and leaves outlined in chain stitch using two strands of S472.

 Left-hand flowerhead outlined in chain stitch using one strand of 4517 (var) with one strand of S606.

Right-hand flowerhead outlined in chain stitch using one strand of E321 with one strand of 4517 (var).

Butterfly

Head and body of butterfly and markings on tail worked in satin stitch using two strands of E130. Feelers worked in backstitch using one strand of E825.

Wings outlined in backstitch using two strands of 4512 (var) with one strand of E825. Large markings on lower wings worked in long and short stitch using two strands of 4512 (var) with one strand of E825, and red dots on tips of lower wings worked in French knots using two strands of S321.

Zigzag markings and blue dots on upper wings worked in satin stitch using two strands of E825; large markings on top of upper wings outlined in chain stitch using two strands of E825 and filled with satin stitch using two strands of 4512 (var).

Arrow patterns on upper wings worked in fly stitch using one strand of S321 with one strand of S606.

Tail outlined in chain stitch using two strands of E825.

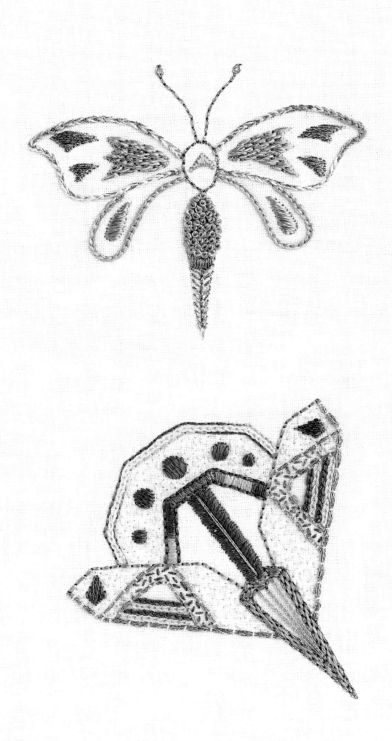

22 Thread key

DMC colours used:

Satin

S307
S367
S3820
S472
S841
S898
S943

Light Effects

E334
E3821
E3843
E746
E825
E898

Stitches and threads used for moth:

Golden yellow ring (body) worked in satin stitch using one strand of E3821 with one strand of S3820. Five gold circles worked in satin stitch using one strand of S3820.

Blue and green markings in lower part of body worked in blanket stitch using two strands of S943 then two strands of E825.

Fine gold lines going across the body and forming the eyes worked in backstitch using two strands of E3821. Eyes worked in French knots using one strand of E3821.

Yellow areas above eyes worked in satin stitch using two strands of S307.

Upper forewing edges worked in satin stitch using two strands of E746.

Lower forewing edges worked in satin stitch using two strands of S943.

Wing patterns worked in fly stitch using two strands of E334; then two strands of E3843; then two strands of E825, working outwards.

Smaller turquoise wings outlined in backstitch using two strands of E334.

Stitches and threads used for grasshopper:

Feelers worked in backstitch using two strands of E3821; eye worked in satin stitch using two strands of E3821.

Legs outlined in backstitch using two strands of E3821.

Head and body outlined in backstitch using two strands of S367. 'V'-shaped marking on body and marking on back leg worked in same way.

Upper back stripes worked downwards in satin stitch using two strands of the following colours: S898; S841; E746, E3821 then E746 again.

Lower back stripes worked in satin stitch using two strands of S898 and E898.

Lower body stripes (from left to right) worked in satin stitch using two strands of S367; two strands of S472; two strands of S841; then two strands of S898.

Tail and tail stripe worked in satin stitch using two strands of E3821.

27 Thread key

DMC colours used:

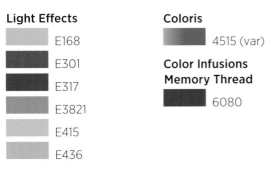

Light Effects

E168
E301
E317
E3821
E415
E436

Coloris

4515 (var)

Color Infusions Memory Thread

6080

Stitches and threads used:

Head and neck outlined in backstitch using one strand of E301 with one strand of E436. Same threads used to fill the head in seed stitch and work the band around neck in satin stitch.

Body, working from top down

Silver hexagon outlined in backstitch using two strands of E415; filled in with straight stitch using one strand of E415. Bolts outlined in satin stitch using two strands of E317; filled in with satin stitch using two strands of E168.

Gold wheel worked in satin stitch using two strands of E3821.

Large gold hexagon worked as for silver hexagon, using two strands of E436 for outline and bolts, and one strand of E436 for the straight stitching.

Tail 'screw' outlined in backstitch using one strand of E301 with one strand of E3821 and filled in with seed stitch using one strand of E301.

Top left limb

Glasses outlined with couching using six strands of E3821 couched with one strand of 4515 (var). Hinge worked in satin stitch using two strands of E436. Reflections worked in backstitch using two strands of E168. Nose pieces worked in French knots using two strands of E168.

Glasses' arm worked in long and short stitch using two strands of 4515 (var). The arm is attached to the body with long and short stitch using one strand of 4515 (var) with one strand of E415.

Middle left limb

Limb and eyelet outlined in backstitch using one strand of E436 with one strand of 4515 (var). Same threads used to work bolts in straight stitch. Fill in the shape by working around the outline, crossing over previous stitches. Bottom edge worked in straight stitch using two strands of E168.

Stripe worked in satin stitch using one strand of E436 with one strand of 4515 (var) then in straight stitch using two strands of E301. Silver screw worked in satin stitch using two strands of E168.

Upper right limb

Outlined in backstitch using one strand of E415 with one strand of 4515 (var). Screw at top and three spikes worked in satin stitch using two strands of E415.

Middle right limb

Outlined in backstitch using two strands of E168. Filled in straight stitch using one strand of E168. Screw worked in satin stitch using two strands of E168.

Lower limbs

Outlined in backstitch using two strands of E317. Screws worked in satin stitch using two strands of E168 or two strands of E317.

Corkscrew worked in satin stitch using two strands of E415 at top, then two strands of E168.

Scissors outlined in backstitch using two strands of E168 (right blade) and two strands of E415 (left). Right handle and screw worked in satin stitch using two strands of E415.

Appliqué coils (optional)

The two coils are worked in couched or appliqué coil, using 6080. For each coil, cut a 20cm (8in) length of memory thread and wrap it around a bodkin, or similar, six to eight times, leaving the ends free. Using a sharp-pointed needle, make a hole in the fabric where you want to insert each end. Enlarge the hole gently with the bodkin. Keeping the coil wrapped on the bodkin, insert the ends into the holes and pull through to the reverse. Bend the ends of the wire over on the reverse and over-sew in place securely. Trim off the excess. Once the design is completed, remove the bodkin.

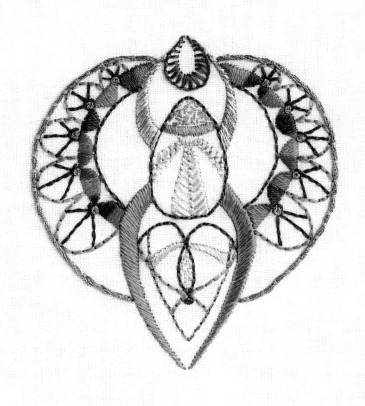

32 Thread key

DMC colours used:

Satin
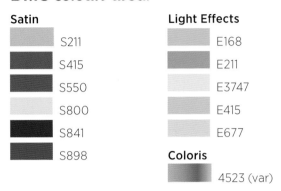

S211

S415

S550

S800

S841

S898

Light Effects

E168

E211

E3747

E415

E677

Coloris

4523 (var)

Stitches and threads used:

Design outline worked in satin stitch using two strands of S898 and two strands of S550, as shown opposite.

Outer flower motif (repeat six times)

Flowerhead loop and stalk worked in chain stitch using two strands of 4523 (var).

Base worked in satin stitch using two strands of S841.

Small detail within flowerhead and base worked in satin stitch using two strands of E677.

Insect motif (repeat six times)

Feelers, forming star pattern in centre of design worked in satin stitch using two strands of 4523 (var).

Mandibles (tiny horns on top of head) worked in satin stitch using two strands of S211.

Head outlined in satin stitch using two strands of E3747. Head filled with satin stitch using two strands of E168; two strands of S415; and two strands of S800.

French knots (eyes) worked using two strands of 4523 (var).

Upper body

Upper body outlined in backstitch using two strands of E168.

Squares worked in satin stitch using two strands of E3747; two strands of S800; two strands of S415 and two strands of E415 as shown.

Three French knots worked below each of the four squares using two strands of 4523 (var) .

Solid shape below French knots worked in satin stitch using two strands of E168.

Wings

Wings outlined in chain stitch using two strands of S211.

Top outer corners of wings worked in long and short stitch using two strands of 4523 (var).

Remaining outer stripes worked in satin stitch using two strands of E677, two strands of 4523 (var) and two strands of S841.

French knots on top inner corners of wings worked using two strands of 4523 (var).

Zigzag patterns worked in satin stitch using two strands of S550.

Spaces between zigzag patterns filled with seed stitch using two strands of E211.

Wing tips shaded in satin stitch using two strands of S898.

Lower body

Bottom edge of body worked in chain stitch using two strands of S800.

T-shirt

Reflective and metallic threads will make your embroidery stand out on a night out.

Denim skirt

Jazz up a plain skirt with a cute, colourful motif – perfect for summer holidays. Adapt some of the elements of the design to add detail around the pockets.

Tabard

Put the fun into 'functional' with one or two bee motifs embroidered onto serviceable clothing.

95

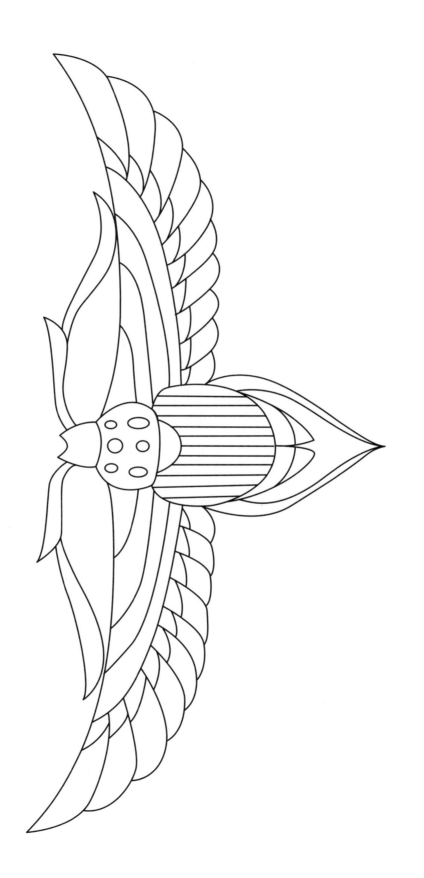

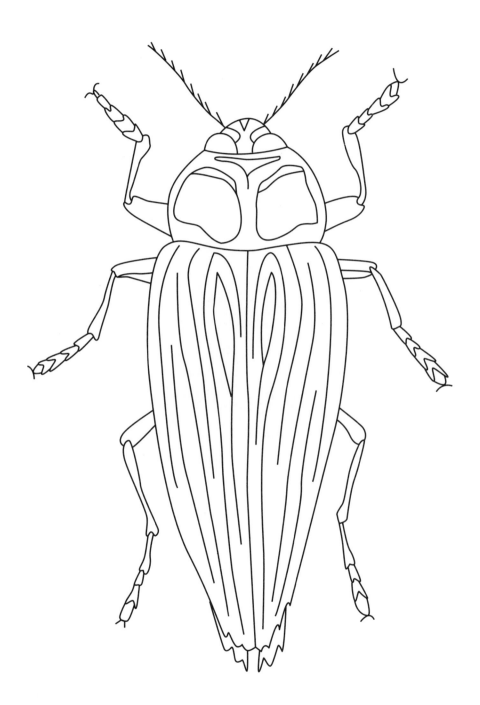

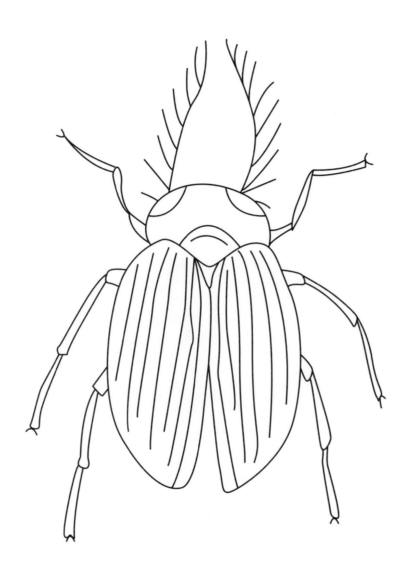

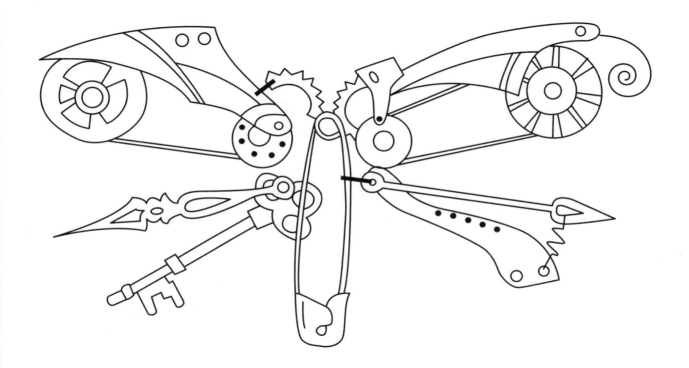

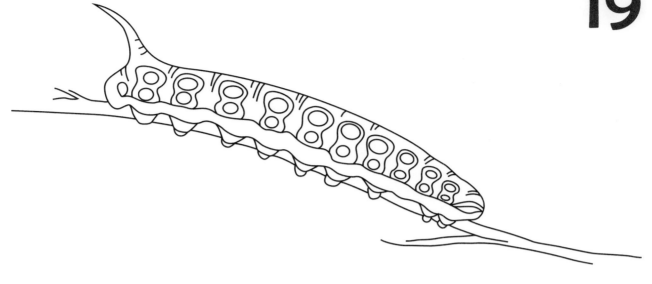

DEFINITIONS

Useful terms to refer to:

Arcane

Mysterious or secret; not understood by many.

Esoteric

As above; mysterious and little-known.

Iconography

The use of images and symbols to convey meanings.

Intuition

The ability to understand something through feeling rather than thinking.

Major Arcana

The twenty-two 'trump cards' of the tarot deck, depicting significant life chapters.

Minor Arcana

The four suits of the tarot deck, depicting more fleeting experiences and feelings.

Occult

Relating to mystical powers or supernatural phenomena.

Oracle

In ancient times, oracles were priests or priestesses who could communicate with the spirit world, interpret mystic symbols and guide truth-seekers in their decisions.

Querent

The person who seeks an answer from a tarot reading. This either refers to you in a reading, or to those you read for.

Spread

In tarot, a spread refers to the way the cards are arranged in a reading.

Unconscious

The part of our minds that affects our feelings and behaviour without us realising it.

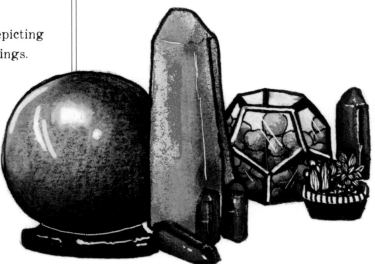

WHAT IS TAROT?

Tarot is a friend to all who know its secrets. Find out how a simple deck of cards can become your coach, your confidant and your counsel.

Tarot cards are a special form of playing card. Unlike a usual deck of cards, they are not used to win at games. Instead, tarot cards exist to be interpreted. They are a tool that can help with solving problems and making decisions, by reflecting back conscious and unconscious thoughts and feelings – like a mirror. In this part of the book, we will explore how tarot works, trace its roots through time and discover its modern uses.

HOW DOES TAROT WORK?

There is a very simple way to find out how tarot works. All you need is a single coin.

It can be any coin. Once you have found one, hold it in your hand and think of a yes/no question. It can be anything – *Do I want to see my friend tomorrow?* Heads means yes, tails means no. Focus on the question and flip the coin. The upwards-facing side of the coin gives you your answer.

How do you feel? Maybe you feel disappointed in the coin's answer. Maybe you feel glad about it. Either way, the coin has answered your question.

The coin is just a coin. It doesn't know the workings of your mind, or your heart's desire.

Equally, what you do next is up to you – in this case, the coin is a prompt, not a command. But the simple act of flipping a coin has done something important. It has shown you how you feel.

Like the coin, tarot helps you conjure up your true feelings.

This is your intuition – the sum of your experiences, your sensations, your feelings. Your intuition is a powerful guide. You can access your intuition at any time and use it to test complex decisions. Sometimes a course of action looks appealing, or seems expected, but does it *feel* right, deep in your belly?

Befriend your cards! Keep them in a special box or wrapped in a piece of silk. Treated with care, they will serve you for a long time, and be there for you in moments of curiosity, self-doubt, confusion and anticipation.

WITHIN THE DECK

Discover the different parts of a typical tarot deck

Major Arcana

The first twenty-two cards of a tarot deck are unique to tarot. Called the Major Arcana, and numbered from zero to twenty-one, these cards look mysterious, and are loaded with meaning. Each card in the Major Arcana represents a major chapter in life – though how you feel about each card may change as often as your circumstances do!

The Major Arcana cards show us emotions and experiences that can shape our lives: grief, hope, joy, confusion, fear, love and more.

They also show us figures who embody powerful roles that are likely to influence us, such as mother (The Empress), father (The Emperor) and teacher (The Hierophant).

THE EMPRESS.

THE EMPEROR.

THE HIEROPHANT.

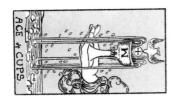

Minor Arcana

The Minor Arcana is the name for the cards in a tarot deck outside of the Major Arcana. There are fifty-six cards in the Minor Arcana, divided across four suits, and they depict a wide array of experience and feelings.

In a reading, the cards of the Minor Arcana can be as influential as those of the Major Arcana, but are tied to more specific circumstances – such as work or learning. The cards of the Minor Arcana describe the passing moods and smaller shifts of our lives.

The Four Suits

The Minor Arcana is made up of four suits, like a pack of playing cards. Like playing cards, each of the four suits has an Ace, a Queen and a King. In the tarot, each suit has a Knight instead of a Jack, and a fourth court card, featuring a youthful Page. In a reading, the Page, Knight, Queen and King cards often represent people in our lives.

Each of the four tarot suits represents a different focus. The Swords (pp.54–61) represent thought, reason and decision-making. Air is the Swords' element. The Pentacles (pp.62–69) – sometimes known as Coins – explore security, wealth and practicality. Their associated element is the earth. The Cups (pp.38–45) represent intuition, emotion and fluidity, and their element is water. Fire belongs to the Wands suit (pp.46–53), which refers to projects, energy and work.

surrender ✳ patience
☾ serenity

The Hanged Man shows us a peaceful-looking person, suspended upside-down from a cross. The figure bears a halo, suggesting enlightenment. The Hanged Man is about letting things be. Sometimes is right to do everything in your power change things. At other times, it is better stop struggling, and just let go. Choosing to accept an imperfect new situation, or to give something you care about, can set you free. y taking this patient approach, you may find at you begin to see things in a new light.

THE HANGED MAN.

DEATH.

13. Death

change ☀ endings
✳ acceptance

A skeleton rides a pale horse, b a victory banner. All fall beneat horse's hooves. When the Death card co in your reading, it is rarely about death it is there to remind us that all things eve come to an end. Maybe a friendship, love or a chapter in your life is ending. Thi affirms the pain that arises when this ha We cope with loss best when we let ou feel it and remember that something ne arise. Look to the sun, rising on the horizon bringing a new day.

14. Temperance

TEMPERANCE.

15. The Devil

THE DEVIL.

health 🌙 *balance*
✳ *moderation*

craving ✳ *weakness*
☀ *isolation*

An angel pours water back and forth between two cups. One foot is in a pool of water, symbolising emotions; the other is on firm ground, symbolising practical needs. Temperance invites us to seek a happy balance in our lives. Recall a time when you felt full of well-being. Perhaps you got plenty of sleep, plenty of food to eat and all was well for you and those you care about. There are no extremes here – Temperance is all about valuing the gentle things that sustain us.

The Devil crouches above two fi[gures] – perhaps The Lovers – who a[re] chains, and subject to his will. In the [...] The Devil is about feeling powerless. M[aybe] you've been feeling pressure to fit in[...] betraying your true values. Maybe y[ou've] been chasing short-term highs and nov[...] empty. Maybe you are putting energy [into] shallow things. Whatever is preoccup[ying] you leaves you feeling bad. This card is [...] to say that what you are experienci[ng is] part of being human. Recognising that [...] is an issue will enable you to make cha[nges]

16. The Tower

THE TOWER.

destruction ☾ *shock*
✴ *change*

The Tower shows a fortress being struck by lightning. Crowned figures fall from the castle walls. Here, The Tower symbolises certainty: the way we tend to assume that things will always be as they seem. The bolt of lightning strikes and shakes the tower, reminding us that nothing is certain, and we are works in progress. A statement like 'I am good at science, but I'm not funny' may *feel* true – but may not always be so. A shock can quickly upend old assumptions. This card prompts you to explore new aspects of yourself, and reveal unexpected possibilities.

17. The Star

THE STAR.

hope ✴ *reassurance*
☀ *renewal*

The figure in this card pours water onto the earth and into a lake. Stars blaze in the clear skies above her, and she is completely at ease in her body. When you are weary, sad and at a low ebb, The Star card brings you solace and says, 'you are okay'. In a reading, this card invites you to connect with things that inspire hope in you. When you feel dull and fed up, do a little of what you love – it will help you revive your sparkle. Think of it like water, springing up through the earth, bringing life back to the land and back to you.

Ace of Wands

ACE of WANDS.

energy ☾ *boldness*
✸ *readiness*

The Wands represent action, and drawing the Ace of Wands is like being given a surge of pure energy. Here you can see that the wand itself is a living thing, budding with green leaves; seize it like the hand in the card is your own! Embrace growth and life's incredible possibilities. You may have cause to hesitate, but this is a trump card: it says, 'Get started – now is the time to make things happen'. This card invites you to rise to a new challenge with confidence.

Two of Wands

self-assurance ✸ *power*
◉ *purpose*

A regal figure holds the world in one hand, a wand in the other, and gazes out to sea. Great things have been accomplished – this is someone who knows his power and what he can do with it. He may even be bored, and in search of fresh challenges that will test him. In a reading, the Two of Wands invites you to feel assured. You've done well – take a look around and enjoy the view. It also calls on you to be inventive and apply yourself to any fresh problems in your life. Let these become your future successes.

Three of Wands

vision ☾ *exploration*
✴ *leadership*

A figure looks out on a stretch of sea where ships sail. Beneath their robes they wear armour – they are ready to take risks. The two wands behind the figure suggest further, unseen, opportunities that have yet to be grasped. The Three of Wands suggests being prepared in a practical sense, but also having vision. What is coming? In a reading, this card encourages you to move out of your comfort zone and seek new adventures. The Three of Wands reminds you that being ready to try something new often results in exciting discoveries.

Four of Wands

celebration ✴ *community*
☀ *delight*

A celebration is underway beyond the confines of the city walls. It could be seasonal or ceremonial; the mood is light and fun-filled. Garlands of flowers decorate the space. This card evokes festivals, parties, weddings, holidays and family feasts – special occasions where people get together for happy reasons and gather as a temporary community outside the routines of daily life. Freedom from restriction is a theme of this card. Such moments are fleeting – the Four of Wands invites you to cut loose, enjoy the day and be jubilant!

Five of Wands

competition ✳ *disagreement*
☾ *teamwork*

Five figures are locked in a tussle – or is it a game? The Five of Wands refers to feeling competitive and taking on your rivals. It can also represent feeling annoyed and having to fight for your rightful place in a group. Maybe a team effort is going wrong, no one is listening and quarrels are surfacing. This card calls on you to engage with disagreements in good spirits. Frustrations are a natural part of teamwork. The question is, what may emerge from the dispute? And what role will you play?

Six of Wands

triumph ☀ *acclaim*
✳ *· flying high*

The Six of Wands is very much a victory card. The battle is over, the contest has been won. A figure rides a horse in a victory procession, wreathed in the laurels that signified glory in Ancient Greece and Rome. This card symbolises great success in your ventures, particularly the kind of success that follows a long struggle. In a reading, it suggests that you've overcome difficulties and at last your talents are being recognised and praised. It can also warn against arrogance. Bask in the recognition coming your way, but don't let it go to your head.

Seven of Wands

being assertive ☾ *defiance*
✴ *firmness*

In life, it can be wise to let things go, and accept a situation. At other times, we must be proactive about sticking up for ourselves. In the Seven of Wands a figure defends themself from challengers. This card invites you to have courage in your convictions and be outspoken. Sometimes asking nicely won't get you anywhere – but expressing yourself firmly and with confidence will. Expect adversity; let your adrenaline energise you. When you confront difficulties head on, it can pay off. Even if it doesn't, you'll know you did your best.

Eight of Wands

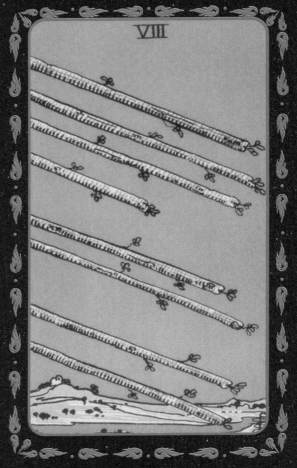

speed· ✴ *motion*
☀ *conclusion*

The Eight of Wands is all about accelerating towards a conclusion. You are in the thick of something and life is busy and exciting – a blur that speeds by. Like the wands in the card, events have been catapulted into motion and will fly through the air until they hit the earth with a bump! In a reading, this card evokes the thrill of feeling inspired, being full of energy and focused on completing a task. It can signify that you are right in the 'flow' of a project or phase and encourages you to embrace and use this intensity to your advantage.

Nine of Wands

Ten of Wands

feeling defensive ☾
pluckiness ✳ *determination*

feeling burdened ✳ *struggle*
☀ *exhaustion*

The man in the Nine of Wands has been through a lot. Covered in bandages, he looks back at the wands resentfully – whilst still being ready for another fight. This card reminds us that arguments take a toll on us. They often leave us feeling touchy and attacked. Yet there can be grace in sticking with the struggle. The Nine of Wands invites you to take stock of your situation and keep seeking resolution if a particular battle really matters to you, even if it causes you discomfort.

A figure works to move an armful of wands forward. Though there is a village on the horizon, where they can lay down their burden and recover, the wands obscure their view. This card warns you that the enthusiastic aspect of the Wands suit can lead you into difficulties: maybe you've felt unable to say no to new demands, and then become exhausted. Your energy is spread too thin, and nothing is coming easily. Put aside some responsibilities and reconnect with whatever brings you joy.

Ace of Pentacles

ACE of PENTACLES.

stability ☽ *protection*
✴ *encouragement*

The Ace of Pentacles suggests that a promising time of well-being and security is within reach. If it comes up in a reading, maybe you'll pick up more hours at that part-time job! Bringing together all the power of the Pentacles suit, this golden ace affirms your trustworthy nature, your dedication to doing a good job — and your ability to flourish as you work towards your goals. There is a contrasting feature in this card: follow the little path through the leafy archway and you'll reach the mountains — a reminder that aiming high requires struggle.

Two of Pentacles

focus ✴ *being interested*
☀ *balance*

A dancing figure expertly juggles two pentacles as ships sail the seas behind him. Wholly absorbed, the juggler is not distracted by the wider world. His pentacles move in an infinite figure-of-eight loop, suggesting a smooth flow of energy, a healthy balance. When you pull the Two of Pentacles in a reading, take a moment to think about your pursuits: how are you using your energy? Are you too busy, or bored? It may be time to seek out activities that give you the focused, contented state of mind that the Two of Pentacles embodies.

Three of Pentacles

teamwork 🌙 *planning*
✴ *achievement*

Some tasks can be done alone. Others require more thought, more skills and more time – which means more people. This card is all about the value of teamwork. Three figures work together – each of their voices and skills are equally valuable, and the pressure is shared between them. In a reading, this card could be a sign that it's time to reach out for help and collaborate. Perhaps you have a group project to work on, or a task that's too big to tackle alone.

Four of Pentacles

saving up ✴ *hoarding*
☀ *insecurity*

A man hugs a pentacle-coin close to his chest. His feet pin two pentacles to the ground and a pentacle crowns him. He is focused on hanging on to whatever he already possesses. This card shows how anxiety can rule us, and feed our materialistic tendencies. Just because you 'have' something, doesn't mean you'll be happy. Note how this man is immobilised by his need to hang on to what he owns. This card counsels you to value what you have without letting it define you. Make use of it and share it with others – being generous opens you up to life

Five of Pentacles

need ✳ *worry*
☾ *disappointment*

Two unhappy figures trudge through the snow on a dark night. One of them uses crutches and is bandaged up. They need rest, warmth and care. They walk alongside a lit-up church – but there is no door. Have they been turned away? Or are they so used to surviving on their own that they don't seek help? Though they need a great deal, they have had to learn how to make do with little. In a reading, this card may reflect your own situation or that of people around you. It can act as a nudge to ask for help, or to look out for those who are experiencing hardship.

Six of Pentacles

power ✹ *wealth*
✳ *dependency*

A wealthy merchant gives coins to a beggar, while another waits in hope. Both crouch at his feet. The merchant holds a scale in one hand; he is judging how much to give, and to who. When we lack money, we rely on others to provide – and this can sometimes come with strings attached: *Do this, do that, don't be ungrateful.* This attitude may be one you may find yourself repeating someday, when your own pockets are full! The Six of Pentacles reminds you that when you can, give to others freely, without expecting something in return.

Seven of Pentacles

Eight of Pentacles

success ◗ *taking stock*
✳ *accomplishment*

skill ✳ *focus*
☀ *determination*

In this card, each pentacle-coin symbolises a task. A young man contemplates them before turning to the last task at his feet: he is taking a moment to enjoy the satisfaction that follows hard work. The Seven of Pentacles focuses on how good it feels to look back at a job well done. This card reminds us to celebrate our successes. Next time you are faced with a long list of things to do, find energy by thinking of the satisfaction that will come after you have ticked them all off!

A young man bends over his work. All of his energy is focused on getting this particular task done, and done well. The pentacles on the post represent everything he has accomplished so far. The Eight of Pentacles is very similar to the Seven, only here we see someone in full flow. This card is about powering through a big project until it is done or repeating a process until you master it. When you draw this card, think about any projects, tasks or skills you're working on and remember that focus and practice makes perfect.

Nine of Pentacles

comfort ☾ *fulfillment* ✳ *plenty*

A graceful woman walks in a lush garden full of ripe fruit and coins – her life is rich and she has everything needs. A falcon rests on her hand – a sign of her command over her life. A homestead is behind her but she is comfortable where she is. Like the snail at her feet, she is self-sufficient. She has accomplished a great deal, and she is now able to enjoy her prosperity and the independence it gives her. In a reading, this card invites you to take pleasure in your successes. Treat yourself and enjoy the rewards of your efforts – you deserve it!

Ten of Pentacles

community ✳ *business-as-usual* ◉ *exchange*

A bustling marketplace reveals a pair of traders, an elderly man, a playful child and begging dogs. The Ten of Pentacles celebrates the exchange of goods, money and wisdom. In some interpretations, the people we see are connected through family ties; in others, they are connected by the bonds of community. This card shows us everyday life when times are good, where the bustle of living alongside others is almost taken for granted. In a reading, you may think of everyday life in your local community, and the traditions you might inherit and choose to observe – or to ignore!

Page of Pentacles

being studious ☾ *humble*
✳ *practical*

PAGE of PENTACLES.

As with all page cards, this young person is a student, seeking a better understanding of their suit. In the case of the Page of Pentacles, this means learning useful skills and developing a positive approach to work. The figure regards the pentacle-coin with curiosity, focus and a calm readiness. They know that patience and effort will be required for them to become successful. The next time you sit down to tackle an assignment that doesn't thrill you, let this page serve as a gentle inspiration to you.

Knight of Pentacles

predictable ✳ *steady*
☀ *reliable*

Of all the knights, the Knight of Pentacles is the least flashy. He keeps watch, and his stillness is matched by both his horse and the land he surveys. More of a guardian than a warrior, he can be depended upon. In fact, he is so reliable, he can be a little bit dull. He doesn't care if he or his ways bore you – he cares about doing things well. In a reading, this knight may represent a person in your life, or he may relate to your own approach to a task. Half of the battle is showing up – and the rest is sticking with it.

KNIGHT of PENTACLES.

THE THREE- CARD SPREAD

A single tarot card tells you something about one particular moment, mood or situation. It's practical, but it can be limiting. When you put tarot cards together in a spread, you will find a whole story that shines a light on your situation.

A THREE-CARD SPREAD is perfect for when you, or your querent, are feeling a bit stuck on an everyday problem. The cards can refresh your thinking and reveal a path forward. There are many ways of doing a three-card reading.

Before you start, decide on a question or problem, then choose a structure for your reading. Here are some example structures:

THE PAST (card 1), THE PRESENT (card 2), THE FUTURE (card 3)

AN ISSUE (card 1), THE CAUSE (card 2), THE SOLUTION (card 3)

YOU (card 1), ANOTHER PERSON (card 2), WHAT MAY HAPPEN (card 3)

GOAL (card 1), OBSTACLE (card 2), ACTION (card 3)

When you're ready, shuffle and draw your cards, interpreting them one at a time. How does each card make you feel? How does each card relate to the structure of the spread? This may not always be clear straight away, so dig deep. Say you draw a card that symbolises the past – does it remind you of someone or something from recent months? Did you once embody the energy of this card? Or perhaps it is the opposite – does the card point to what was *missing* from your past? Look for what resonates with you.

When all three cards are facing up, what story do you feel they tell? And what will you do now?

77

THE CELTIC CROSS SPREAD

This ten-card spread is perfect for when you want to try an in-depth tarot reading, either for yourself or for others. Use it to dig deeply into a more specific dilemma, for example: *'What should I do about [a particular situation]?'*

Key:

1. That Which Covers You – you and your situation
2. That Which Crosses You – an obstacle blocking your path
3. A Conscious Thought – something on your mind; a known factor
4. The Past – a circumstance that brought you here
5. Root Cause – the unexplored foundation of your dilemma
6. The Future – new circumstances that will emerge
7. You & Your Role – your current state of mind
8. That Which Surrounds You – your environment, i.e. the people around you, and where you spend your time
9. Hopes & Fears – can also be Hopes OR Fears
10. Outcome – where your situation may take you

Shuffle the cards as you ponder your dilemma. If you're reading for someone else, encourage your querent to shuffle and talk through their dilemma with you.

Take the cards and fan them out face-down, then draw or ask the querent to draw out ten cards. Once ten cards have been drawn, you can arrange them into the layout shown opposite.

When ready to start, turn over the card in the no. 1 position, and, if you're reading for someone else, explain the card to your querent. Ask them for their thoughts and listen to their answer. If you're reading for yourself, examine your own thoughts and feelings in response to each card.

As with the three-card spread, consider each card in relation to its position. Examine your first reaction, look up the card's meaning, and think about where it has appeared in the spread. Then make an interpretation about how it connects to your situation.

Repeat the process until all ten cards are visible. Consider the story that the cards are telling. How do you or your querent feel about it? A full celtic cross spread can take up to one hour to read.

BEYOND THE BOOK

You have started on a journey of discovery, truth-seeker –
and though this book ends here, the journey goes on. You are
now equipped with knowledge that will serve you well as you
explore tarot for yourself and with others. Seek out those
who share your curiosity, and learn from each other as you
become practised in the art of reading these precious cards.

Knowing what you now know about tarot can bring you
clarity, insight and wisdom throughout your life. As you
experience all that living can offer, from love to loss and
everything in between, remember that the cards will always
be there, ready for whenever you need them.

Introduction

Recent initiatives in mathematics teaching emphasise the importance of mathematical discussion within problem-solving, and within mathematical learning generally. Children learn maths by doing it and talking about it, hence language is integral to securing mathematical learning. The activities in this book require children to focus on speaking and listening, and on reasoning, as they interpret clues and identify which items to eliminate.

When we talk, we engage in dialogue with others, and we receive feedback from them. We want children to be involved in mathematical dialogue to help them explore, investigate, challenge, evaluate and actively construct mathematical meaning. When children work together in a small group, they can articulate their thinking, listen to one another and support each other's learning in a safe situation. Organising problem-solving in small groups increases the potential for developing the skills of speaking, listening and working together.

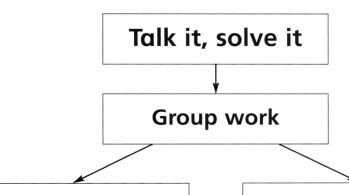

Talk it, solve it

↓

Group work

Speaking and listening
- asking relevant questions to clarify
- making contributions relevant to the topic
- qualifying or justifying ideas
- responding to others appropriately, taking into account what they say

Reasoning skills
- being strategic
- finding examples to match a statement
- being systematic
- looking for patterns
- looking for ways to overcome difficulties
- checking results

The 'Talk it, solve it' activities

In these activities, children identify an unknown item (number, shape, amount, and so on) by means of clues, or questions and answers.

Each unit contains:

- a 'Solve it' sheet giving a collection of eight items, one of which is the unknown item.

- a 'Talk it' sheet with eight clues. These clues give enough information (and more) to identify this unknown item.

- an 'Ask it' sheet with a set of questions. Children choose their own item for others to identify, and the rest of the group ask the questions to discover the unknown item. Some of the questions are deliberately left open by including a blank space where children can insert their own number, shape, amount or other item.

The first unit consists of the 'Solve it' sheet, three different 'Talk it' clue sheets, and an 'Ask it' sheet. This unit will enable you to introduce the activity to the whole class, and to give the class confidence in using clues logically and effectively.

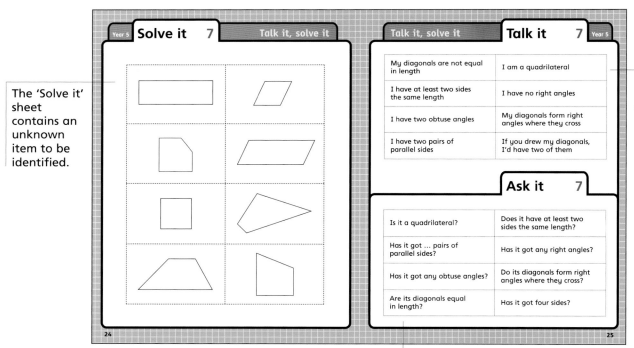

The 'Solve it' sheet contains an unknown item to be identified.

The 'Talk it' sheet contains clues to the identity of the unknown item.

The 'Ask it' sheet contains questions for use in group work.

Introducing the activity to the whole class

The 'Talk it' and 'Solve it' sheets

Display the 'Solve it' sheet on the whiteboard or overhead projector. Alternatively, if these are not available, give each pair of children a copy of the 'Solve it' sheet. Look at the numbers (or other items) shown and invite the children to identify some of the properties of the numbers. Support their observations by asking questions such as "Do you think that number is in the 5 times table? I wonder if there are any other numbers in that table?"

Display the 'Talk it' sheet, look at the clues shown and talk about them briefly, or read out each statement in turn. You may choose to use the opportunity to check that children understand the mathematical content of the clues. Discuss with the class how to use these statements to eliminate items on the 'Solve it' sheet.

Choose one statement from the 'Talk it' sheet and cross out any eliminated items on the 'Solve it' sheet as they are identified. Continue like this until there is one item left. Go through any remaining clues as a check. If any statements don't fit, challenge the class to redress this or rethink.

The answers to the 'Solve it' sheets can be found on page 36 (for Year 5) and on page 64 (for Year 6).

The 'Ask it' sheet

Display the 'Ask it' sheet and read through the questions. Tell the children you are going to think of an item on the 'Solve it' sheet. They must ask you questions to discover the item you have secretly chosen. Discuss with the children which items to eliminate from the 'Solve it' sheet for each question.

When they have worked out your item, invite a pair of children to choose a secret item from the 'Solve it' sheet. Other pairs decide which questions to ask to find out the secret item. Talk with the children about the best questions to ask.

Working in pairs or small groups

Each group will need the 'Solve it' sheet to share between them, and the 'Talk it' sheet cut into strips. Ask the children to take it in turns to choose a 'Talk it' strip, read it to the group and together decide which item to eliminate on the 'Solve it' sheet. The children should keep taking turns until they have only one item left on the 'Solve it' sheet. Extend the activity by asking the group to establish if all the

'Talk it' statements are equally important. Ask if some statements eliminate more possibilities than others. Ask how few statements they can use to solve the problem. These questions could be used as a basis for a plenary discussion.

Meeting diverse needs

Children who need additional support

The activity can be adapted for children who need additional support by asking them to take a 'Talk it' strip and match it to one of the items on the 'Solve it' sheet. The activity then becomes one of identifying properties of a number, shape or other item.

For those who can manage a further challenge, put the cut 'Talk it' strips in a pile and invite children to pick the top one from the pile. Talk this through to decide which items it could refer to. Dealing with one clue at a time is simpler for inexperienced children than choosing a strip from the complete range.

More able learners

Suggest that children explore which of the 'Talk it' statements is the most informative and eliminates most items. When they have identified the unknown item on the 'Solve it' sheet, they should try again and find how many different routes there are through to that solution, including the shortest and the longest.

Invite them to invent their own questions as well as using those on the 'Ask it' sheet. Pairs can invent their own 'Solve it' sheet and a set of clues for other pairs to solve.

Those learning English as an additional language

Adapt the activity by helping children to organise themselves. Provide two sheets of paper labelled 'maybe' and 'no'. Cut the 'Solve it' sheet into eight pieces and put them all on the 'maybe' paper. Then, as the 'Talk it' clues are read out, children can move the 'Solve it' items on to the 'no' paper.

Setting up the activity in this way provides a lot of helpful repetitious questions and statements.

Using the CD-ROM

The CD-ROM contains all the activity sets in the book. You can either project individual pages onto a whiteboard from your computer or print them out onto acetate sheets and use them on an overhead projector. You can also print the sheets out from the CD rather than making photocopies.

Talk it 3

I am a number between one thousand and one thousand one hundred	I am not a palindromic numeral
My tens digit is even	The sum of my digits is less than fifteen
Add two of my digits together and the answer is 6	Divide me by 10 and there is a remainder
Count in 15s from 1000 and you won't say my name	I do not have two zeros

Ask it 3

Is it a number between … and … ?	Is it a palindromic numeral?
Is the … digit even?	Is the … digit odd?
Is the sum of its digits more than … ?	Is the sum of its digits less than … ?
If it is divided by 10 is there a remainder?	Does it have more than one zero?

2490	2499
2468	2500
2457	2463
2345	3456

Talk it 4

My digits are not arranged in ascending order	I am not 25 times 100
I am between 2000 and 2500	I am less than 249 × 10
I am not a multiple of 10	If you divide me by 10, the answer is more than 246
I am less than two thousand four hundred and sixty-five	I am an odd number

Ask it 4

Are the digits arranged in ascending order?	Is 6 one of its digits?
Is it less than 10 × … ?	Is it less than … × 10?
Is it between … and … ?	Is it a multiple of 10?
If you divide it by 10, is the answer more than … ?	Is it an odd number?

10%	$\dfrac{15}{100}$
100%	$\dfrac{1}{4}$
$\dfrac{1}{100}$	75%
25%	20%

Talk it 5

I am greater than 1%	I am less than one whole
I am between 11% and 81%	I am not equal to twenty hundredths
I am greater than 10%	I am not 15%
I am not equal to one tenth	I am worth more than one quarter

Ask it 5

Is it greater than 1%?	Is it greater than …%?
Is it less than 90%?	Is it less than …%?
Is it equal to … ?	Is it between … and … ?
Is it shown as a percentage?	Is it shown as a fraction, in hundredths?

E	F
I	O
H	N
T	L

Talk it 6

At least two of my lines are parallel to each other	I have fewer than three vertical lines
Some of my lines are perpendicular to each other	If you rotate me through 180 degrees I will look different
I am made up of straight lines	I do not have three parallel lines
I have at least one horizontal line	I have more horizontal lines than vertical lines

Ask it 6

Is it made up of straight lines?	Has it got any horizontal lines?
Has it got more than one vertical line?	Has it got more than one horizontal line?
Has it got more horizontal lines than vertical lines?	Are any of its lines parallel to each other?
Are any of its lines perpendicular to each other?	If I rotate it through 180 degrees, will it look different?

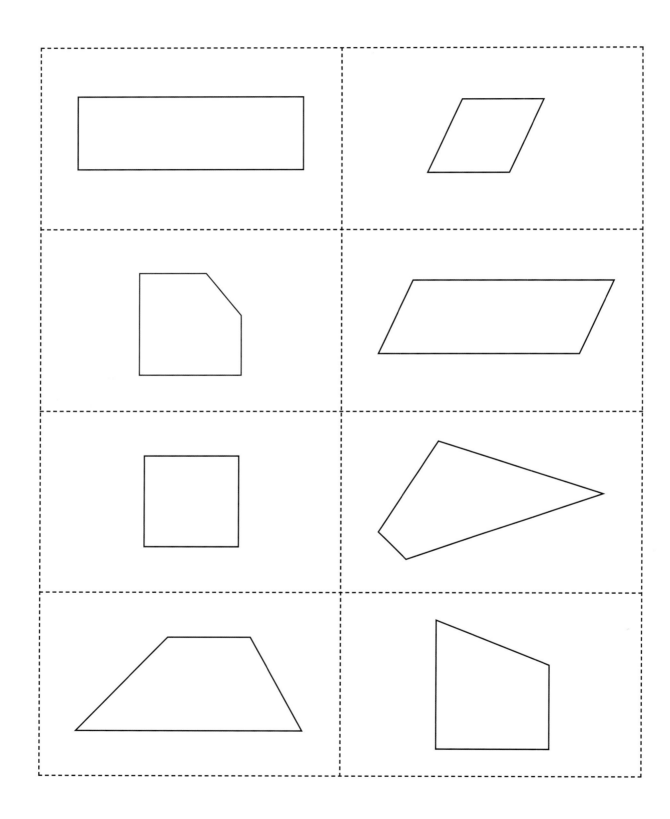

Year 6

Unit 1

Properties of number

Unit 1 consists of the 'Solve it' sheet, three different 'Talk it' clue sheets and an 'Ask it' sheet. This unit will enable you to introduce the activity to the whole class, and to give the class confidence in using clues logically and effectively.

36	144
49	64
100	400
84	121

I am a square number	I am more than the product of 7 and 8
6^2 is less than me	I am not 20^2
I am less than $5 \times 5 \times 5$	4 is one of my factors
A number under 10 was squared to make me	The sum of my digits is not a square number

Talk it 1b

I am more than $4 \times 4 \times 4$	A two-digit number was squared to make me
I am less than the product of 72 and 2	I am greater than the sum of 6^2 and 5^2
The sum of my digits is less than 5	The sum of my digits is a square number
I am not a palindromic numeral	Two of my digits are the same

I am not worth fifty-six hundredths	I am not worth three tenths
I am worth less than 0.56	I am smaller than 70%
I am worth less than 60%	I am bigger than 30%
I am bigger than a half	If you turned me into a fraction, I couldn't be an exact number of tenths

Ask it 6

Is it worth less than …%?	Is it worth less than … ?
Is it worth more than …%?	Is it more than … hundredths?
Is it more than a half?	Is it worth … hundredths?
Is it worth … tenths?	If you turned it into a fraction, could it be an exact number of tenths?

6	23
10	5
24	3
11	q

Talk it   7   Year 6

I am greater than the mode of these numbers: 5, 6, 4, 5, 5, 3, 2, 5, 6, 6	I am less than the mean of: 10, 11, 12
I am inside the range 8–20	I am greater than the mean of these numbers: 4, 6, 8
I am less than the mode of: 11, 21, 30, 18, 11	I am not the mode of: 7, 9, 9, 3, 9
I am in the range 5–25	I am not 3

Ask it   7

Is it more than the mode of these numbers: 7, 10, 9, 11, 10, 9, 4, 10?	Is it less than the mode of these numbers: 11, 21, 30, 18, 11?
Is it less than the mean of: 8, 9, 10?	Is it greater than the mean of: 2, 3, 4?
Is it the mode of: 11, 7, 12, 11, 11?	Is it inside the range 0–6?
Is it in the range … ?	Is it … ?

Talk it 12

My time is more than a year	My time is less than a millennium
My time is less than a century	My time is more than half a decade
My time is not a whole number of years	My time is less than 100 months
My time is less than a decade	The number of my months is a multiple of 5

Ask it 12

Is it ... than a year?	Is it ... than a millennium?
Is it ... than a century?	Is it ... than half a decade?
Is it ... than a decade?	Is it less than ... months?
Is it a whole number of years?	Is the number of months a multiple of ... ?

Answers   Year 6

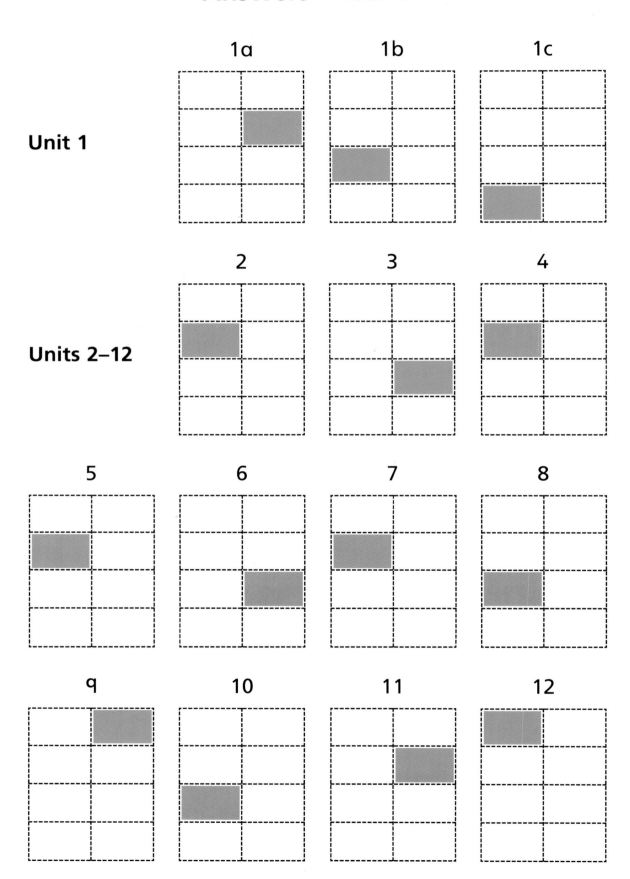

Unit 1

1a   1b   1c

Units 2–12

2   3   4

5   6   7   8

q   10   11   12